How will the world end?

And other questions about the last
things and the second coming of Christ

Jeramie Rinne

thegoodbook
COMPANY

How will the world end?
And other questions about the last things and the second coming of Christ
© Jeramie Rinne/The Good Book Company, 2014
Reprinted 2014

Published by
The Good Book Company
Tel (UK): 0333 123 0880
Tel (North America): (1) 866 244 2165
International: +44 (0) 208 942 0880
Email (UK): info@thegoodbook.co.uk
Email (North America): info@thegoodbook.com

Websites
UK & Europe: www.thegoodbook.co.uk
North America: www.thegoodbook.com
Australia: www.thegoodbook.com.au
New Zealand: www.thegoodbook.co.nz

ISBN: 9781909559653

Printed in the UK by CPI Group (UK) Ltd, Croydon, CR0 4YY
Design by André Parker

Contents

Why is it all so complicated?

t's the end of the world as we know it, and I feel confused.

Where were you when you first realized the world might end? I was a pre-teen, at home, watching television.

I happened upon a program that dramatized what the Bible said would occur in the "end times." Terrifying images crossed the screen: warfare, natural disasters, and, of course, grainy footage of atomic mushroom clouds. I can't remember what the show taught exactly, but I do remember that it scared me.

My next brush with the apocalypse (end of the world) came as a teenager in a church youth group. We saw a film entitled *A Thief in the Night*. In it an unfortunate young woman ignores her family and friends who urge her to follow Jesus. Suddenly the true believers are whisked away in a secret "rapture" up to heaven, leaving her to face the horrific global tribulation (period of suffering) of the last days. On the one hand, the film stoked my curiosity. *What would it be like if millions of people disappeared all at once?* But the film also made me nervous. *Would I be one of the people who gets beamed up by Jesus before the world goes to pieces, or would I be left behind?*

And then there was my youth leader. During a Sunday-school class he explained the biblical teaching about the end of the world using a time line. Actually, it looked more like an electrical-wiring diagram. There were arrows and boxes and symbols all mapping out a complex cascade of final events, like the rapture, the seven-year tribulation, the millennium and the white-throne judgment.

He introduced me to characters from the book of Revelation like the beast and his sidekick, the false prophet, both of whom would serve the dragon by presiding over a one-world government that somehow featured Europe, Russia and China quite prominently. This was after the beast was assassinated and then miraculously revived thee-and-a-half years into the tribulation, of course.

Like *A Thief in the Night*, that teaching had a contradictory effect on me. At one level, it intrigued me. It was like learning a top-secret code that suggested I could decipher the true meaning of current events. But the explanations and charts also confused me with their sheer complexity. Furthermore, how exactly did my youth leader see those things in the Bible? The book of Revelation mystified me, but somehow he could make perfectly good sense of its apocalyptic visions. And on top of it all, that sense of dread and foreboding still seemed to haunt any discussion of the world's grand finale.

Two common reactions

In talking with followers of Jesus about the end of the world, I have found that many suffer from this same jumble of reactions that I experienced: fascination mixed with confusion tinged by fear. As a result, Christians tend to react in one of two ways to the question: *how will the world end?*

Some (a minority it seems) respond by plunging head first into the deep end of the last-days swimming pool. They try to decode the Bible's strange visions, crunch the mysterious numbers, and draw the charts.

These end-time experts understand the differences between terms like pre-tribulational and post-tribulational. They know which "trib" is correct and which Bible verses prove it. They track world events closely, especially events in the Middle East, and they can effortlessly relate those events back to specific Bible prophecies.

But in my experience, far more Christians react to end-of-the-world talk by lurching in the opposite direction. They mostly avoid the topic. They occasionally take off their shoes, roll up their jeans and tentatively dip a toe in the shallow end of apocalyptic speculation. Perhaps they read one of the *Left Behind* books, or sit through a Sunday-school class on the Old Testament book of Daniel. But that's as far as they'll go. Once the conversation starts getting a little deep, they hop out of the pool.

If you ask one of these types if he is a pre-millennialist or a post-millennialist, he might spout the old quip: "I'm a pan-millennialist. It will all pan out in the end!" Or he might give you a two-word interpretation of the book of Revelation: "God wins!" End of discussion.

Why do Bible-believing Christians avoid these parts of their Bibles? Why don't they study more about the end of the world? There are probably several reasons:

- **The end of the world is disputed.** Very smart, devout Christians disagree about end-times stuff. Bible-believing scholars hold widely differing interpretations. If those guys can't agree on what the end-times prophecies mean, how could regular Christians like me possibly sort things out?

- **The end of the world can be divisive.** Even worse, Christians get into arguments about these issues, churches occasionally divide, and in some cases believers doubt the authenticity of one another's faith because of their views. Why risk conflict over something so confusing?

- **The end of the world is uncertain.** We don't know with 100% certainty how every detail will play out until after it happens. So why waste time and energy studying, or fighting about, something so speculative?

- **The end of the world seems irrelevant.** If you believe in Jesus, and you believe that believing in

Jesus is the way to eternal life, then why sweat the details? What if you develop an intricate theory about the end of the world that turns out to be wildly inaccurate? It won't affect your eternal destiny if you trust in Christ. Isn't talking about the end ultimately a distraction from more important truths and from living the Christian life?

Studying the end of the world seems like a lot of work with little payoff. It's just way too complicated, isn't it?

Behold, the forest!

When the details overwhelm you, it's time to step back and see the big picture. Don't lose the forest for the trees. And when it comes to the Bible's teaching about the end of the world, it's easy to study the trees so closely that you get lost in the woods.

This book's primary purpose is to help regular Christians regain that big picture about the end of the world. It's a book about seeing the whole forest once again, not a microscopic study of tree bark. Or switching back to the swimming-pool illustration, this book will not take you on a deep dive to the bottom of the pool to study the tile work around the drain. Rather, this book is intended to help Christians go past their ankles, get wet, and learn to enjoy swimming in the topic without drowning.

I hope this book will help you move from being confused about the end times to having a basic, common-sense understanding. I trust it will free you from fear and anxiety, and enable you to find joy and peace in thinking about the end of the world. Christians should not dread what the Bible says about the end. They should glory in it.

I doubt everyone will agree with everything in this book. I have my own beliefs about the end of the world, and I will attempt to present other views fairly. But my goal isn't so much to focus on the nitty-gritty questions that divide people as it is to highlight the Bible's central teachings about the end, teachings which should bring Christians together rather than separate them into camps. And who knows? Maybe a few end-time junkies will come up from the bottom of the pool while reading this book and take a much needed breath.

And the key to all this—to seeing the forest and to swimming without drowning—is always staying focused on the central figure at the end of the world.

The key is to keep our eyes fixed on Jesus.

Chapter 1

How will the world end?

Coming to a theater near you: *The Apocalypse.*

The end of the world has been big business for Hollywood. Film makers have used advances in computer-generated images to craft a steady stream of apocalyptic-disaster flicks. These jaw-dropping special effects, seen by millions of movie-goers, portray a number of different ways in which the world might get trashed.

For starters, there is the asteroid scenario, depicted in films like *Armageddon* and *Deep Impact.* Massive space-rocks crash into the planet, wiping out cities, spawning towering tsunamis, and threatening humanity with an epic "E.L.E." (extinction level event). In the real world, large asteroids have hit the earth before, and astronomers warn it could happen again.

And then there's the solar flare version: the sun burps

out an enormous wave of radiation that cooks the earth. That's how the world ends in *Knowing* as well as in *2012*, as predicted by the Mayan calendar, of course.

Or perhaps humanity will die at its own hands through pollution and global warming (as in *The Day After Tomorrow* or *Wall-E*), or through the creation of artificial intelligence that turns on its maker like Frankenstein's monster (see *The Terminator* and *The Matrix* series for more details). Or maybe we will get erased by some viral pandemic (as in *Outbreak*, *Contagion* or *12 Monkeys*). And what if that disease turns us into... zombies? Hey, it happened in *World War Z* and *I Am Legend*!

And let us not forget Hollywood's most popular flavor of world catastrophe: the alien invasion. Ever since H.G. Wells' classic *The War of the Worlds*, story-tellers have been asking: "What if we're not alone in the universe, and what if our stellar neighbors aren't nice?" The list of extra-terrestrial-onslaught flicks is far too long to number. Which one is your favorite?

But when we look to the Bible to see how the world will end, we find something completely unexpected. Our doom won't come from asteroids or robots or viruses or aliens. The end of the world will come from something Hollywood never imagined.

A lamb.

I watched as he opened the sixth seal. There was a great earthquake. The sun turned black like sackcloth made of goat hair, the whole moon turned blood red, and the stars in the sky fell to earth, as figs drop from a fig tree when shaken by a strong wind. The heavens receded like a scroll being rolled up, and every mountain and island was removed from its place.

Then the kings of the earth, the princes, the generals, the rich, the mighty, and everyone else, both slave and free, hid in caves and among the rocks of the mountains. They called to the mountains and the rocks, "Fall on us and hide us from the face of him who sits on the throne and from the wrath of the Lamb! For the great day of their wrath has come, and who can withstand it?"

Revelation 6 v 12-17

Before we talk about the Lamb specifically, let's go back to our basic question. Based on this text, how will the world end?

The world will end in judgment

The problem facing the human race is not that it's on a collision course with an asteroid. Our problem is far worse: we are on a collision course with a holy God who is coming to judge a sinful world. From the great moments of judgment in the Old Testament to the messages of Israel's prophets to the teaching of Jesus to the letters of the apostles, the entire Bible warns that this rebellious creation will answer to its Creator.

Notice all the judgment language in these verses. First, we find unnerving depictions of an unraveling universe: the sun goes black, the moon red, stars fall, the sky rolls up, and mountains and islands get deleted. We might wonder to what extent these calamities will literally happen, and to what extent these images are figurative. But the important thing to know is that these words are inspired by Old Testament images describing God's judgment. For example, Isaiah warns of the Lord's coming judicial wrath against all nations. In that warning he says:

> All the stars in the sky will be dissolved and the heavens rolled up like a scroll; all the starry host will fall like withered leaves from the vine, like shriveled figs from the fig tree.
>
> *Isaiah 34 v 4*

When God comes to judge, the world falls apart. The Creator de-creates his creation.

Second, we see judgment imagery in Revelation 6 when the people of earth cower before "him who sits on the throne." God is the King on heaven's throne, and kings in the ancient world acted as judges. Kings made the laws, issued verdicts, and handed out the consequences. So a reference to God's throne would imply judgment, just as a reference to the "bench" would today. The world will end when God calls his Supreme Court to session.

Third, this terrible event is called "the great day of their wrath." We sometimes get stuck on the word "wrath." When we think of wrath, we might imagine an angry drunk cursing and picking fights, or a stressed-out motorist weaving aggressively in traffic while screaming at other drivers, or a hyped-up protestor shouting and shaking his fist, caught up in a dangerous mob mentality. Is God like that? Out of control and out of his mind with fury? Doesn't the Bible say that God is love?

Yes, God is love. But he is also holy. That means God is so pure and good that he hates all sin and evil and wrongdoing. We dislike some sin, particularly when people do bad things that hurt us. But we tend not to think our own sin is that bad. But God is the perfect judge who sees all the evidence and is appalled by it all: lies, gossip, abuse, greed, theft, pride, lust, adultery, abortion, exploitation, cheating, vanity, self-righteousness, idolatry, addiction, selfishness, boasts, and more.

And so God responds with judicial wrath. God's wrath is his perfect, balanced, just disdain of sin that results in fitting judgment. Wrath is the appropriate response of the holy Judge to a world that holds him and his laws in contempt.

Could you imagine if God never judged sin and evil in the world? What if human history went on and on forever, with all the terrible things that people have done to each other, and all the ways that people have ignored Jesus, and God never did anything about it? Wouldn't it in fact be unloving for God not to address sin with judgment and set things right? In what sense could we say that God is "good" if he tolerates evil forever? It would be like a police officer who gave up chasing the bad guys, or a mom who never disciplined her children. The mom might seem loving at first because her kids got whatever they wanted. But in the long run those children would grow up to be spoiled brats, bringing misery on themselves and everyone else around them. An all-powerful God who never brings justice is neither good nor loving.

What a contrast there is between Hollywood and the Bible! In the movie versions of the apocalypse, humanity is usually threatened by natural disasters: solar flares and viruses and, yes, even aliens. In these versions, the apocalypse is just a bit of cosmic bad luck, not a punishment for our wrongs. But the Bible sees the end of the world not as a natural disaster but as a moral disaster. The end comes when the divine Judge interrupts history in direct response to our hearts, words and deeds.

In fact, did you notice what humanity says in the Revelation passage? They call to the rocks and mountains: "Fall on us and hide us!" (6 v 16) The people actually plead for death by natural disaster. Being killed by an asteroid or tsunami or plague will be far more attractive than facing our holy Maker on the day of his wrath.

That judgment will be inescapable

The Hollywood version of the end of the world also differs from the Bible because typically the movie heroes somehow survive the world's end.

In *Armageddon*, a fearless crew shuttles up to an inbound asteroid, drills a shaft, inserts a nuke, and detonates the rock at the last second, saving the planet. In *Independence Day*, a gutsy pilot infiltrates and blows up an alien mother ship at the brink of human extinction. Of course, these movies still provide plenty of global mayhem. But people somehow escape in the end because of their ingenuity, courage and willpower. As one character in *Pacific Rim* defiantly yells: "Today we are cancelling the apocalypse!"

But in the biblical account, humanity does not fare so well. No one escapes God's judgment. Again, look at the list of people affected by the coming day of wrath:

> Then the kings of the earth, the princes, the generals, the rich, the mighty, and everyone else, both slave and free, hid in caves and among the rocks of the mountains. *Revelation 6 v 15*

That list includes, well, everyone. No exceptions. Also, if you go back and count, there are seven types or categories of people listed. The book of Revelation loves symbolic numbers, and the number seven is a favorite. Seven usually indicates totality and completeness, as in the seven days of creation. So the fact that there are seven types of people listed further emphasizes that everybody must face God's wrath.

The Lamb will do the judging

But it is not only the wrath of him who sits on the throne that threatens the entire human race. We will also feel the wrath of the Lamb.

You've probably never put the words "wrath" and "lamb" together in a sentence. Lambs are cute and cuddly, not fiery and furious. People tend not to fear imminent doom while watching a baby sheep frolic in a meadow. But at the end of the world, people will prefer death by avalanche over facing the Lamb's fury.

Who is this Lamb? The "Lamb" is the book of Revelation's code name for Jesus. In Revelation, Jesus is the judging Lamb, who opens the scrolls of judgment, conquers an unbelieving world, and even oversees the eternal judgment of hell.

But maybe that explanation causes even more confusion. Maybe it's just as hard to imagine Jesus judging the world as it is to imagine a wrathful Lamb wiping us out. Perhaps you mainly think of Jesus as kind and gentle, a lover and not a fighter, a friend of sinners rather than their executioner. It is true: Jesus came in obscurity at his birth, ministered among the lowly, and died on a disgraceful cross. But when he comes again, it will be as the glorious Judge, not the tender babe in a manger.

When we look at the rest of the New Testament, we find the same expectation: Jesus will bring final judgment upon the world. For example, the apostle Peter said:

> [Jesus] commanded us to preach to the people and to testify that he is the one whom God appointed as judge of the living and the dead.
>
> *Acts 10 v 42*

And Paul, his fellow apostle, agreed:

> For we must all appear before the judgment seat of Christ, so that each of us may receive what is due to us for the things done while in the body, whether good or bad.
>
> *2 Corinthians 5 v 10*

And where did Peter and Paul get this idea? Jesus himself said so!

> The Father judges no one, but has entrusted all judgment to the Son, that all may honor the Son just as they honor the Father.
>
> *John 5 v 22-23*

At the center of the Bible, and at the center of the whole human story, stands Jesus Christ, the Son of God. And it will be Jesus himself who brings the world to its end. All eyes will be fixed on Jesus the Lamb when he returns as the divine magistrate.

A glimmer of hope

One final thought: there is an upside to Jesus being the Lamb. It is precisely his identity as the Lamb that gives us a glimmer of hope that we might escape the Lamb's wrath.

> "For you [Jesus] were slain, and with your blood you purchased for God persons from every tribe and language and people and nation."
>
> *Revelation 5 v 9*

On the cross Jesus died as the sacrificial Lamb of God in order to ransom sinful people out of the final judgment day. By his own death he absorbed the judicial wrath of God that we deserve. He paid the price so that we could go free. When Jesus was crucified, the sky turned black and the ground shook because end-of-the-world judgment was showing up ahead of time on Jesus, so that those who believe in him might be forgiven and escape humanity's final sentence. The people in Revelation 6 cry out: "The great day of their wrath has come, and who can withstand it?" Here's the answer: those who repent and believe in Jesus Christ, the Lamb of God, will stand.

There's no getting around Jesus, and there's no getting around the final judgment. The only question is whether we will turn to Jesus now as the Lamb who ransoms us, or whether we will face him as the wrathful Lamb on the last day. Will the Lamb carry your judgment for you today, or will he deal it out to you when the world ends?

Why is it taking so long?

It has been two millennia, give or take a century, since Jesus and his apostles warned that the world would end with the return of Jesus to judge the world. So what is the hold-up? Why hasn't he come back yet?

The problem becomes even more glaring because Jesus and his apostles seemed to talk about the end as something really close at hand. After describing the events leading up to his second coming, Jesus said: "Truly I tell you, this generation certainly will not pass away until all these things have happened" (Matthew 24 v 34). Jesus' close friend and follower John said: "Children, this is the last hour" (1 John 2 v 18), and the apostle Peter said: "The end of all things is near" (1 Peter 4 v 7). The British philosopher Bertand Russell wrote an essay in

1927 entitled *Why I Am Not a Christian*. And one of the many reasons why Russell rejected Christianity was because it seemed Jesus and his pals got the timing wrong for doomsday. Russell died in 1970 and Jesus still hasn't come back.

The question isn't new. People raised it back in the time of the New Testament. The same Peter who said that the end was near also addressed the skeptics:

> Above all, you must understand that in the last days scoffers will come, scoffing and following their own evil desires. They will say, "Where is this 'coming' he promised? Ever since our ancestors died, everything goes on as it has since the beginning of creation." *2 Peter 3 v 3-4*

So how did Peter explain the delay?

> But they deliberately forget that long ago by God's word the heavens came into being and the earth was formed out of water and by water. By these waters also the world of that time was deluged and destroyed. By the same word the present heavens and earth are reserved for fire, being kept for the day of judgment and destruction of the ungodly.
> But do not forget this one thing, dear friends: With the Lord a day is like a thousand years, and a thousand years are like a day. The Lord is not slow in keeping his promise, as some understand slowness. Instead he is patient with you, not wanting anyone to perish, but everyone to come to repentance.
> *2 Peter 3 v 5-9*

Peter offered three arguments to skeptics back then, and they apply today as well.

- *God has judged the world before.* Peter reminded them that God judged the world with water during Noah's day. People probably scoffed at Noah and his ark too... until the flood waters came. Peter's point is that God did it before and he will do it again, except that next time he will use fire instead of water!

- *God reckons time differently.* God is eternal. So the time references like "soon" and "near" mean something different to God than they do to us. It's kind of like how waiting an hour seems like an eternity to a 5-year-old, but it's not a big deal to a 90-year-old. So let's do the math: if one thousand years equals one day to God, then from God's perspective we're just at about day three since Peter said: "The end of all things is near."

- *God is being patient for our sake.* God has delayed the judgment to give the world time to repent of its sin and turn to Jesus. The lag in Jesus' return shows how loving, patient and merciful God is. We who trust in Jesus need to make the most of this time to tell the gospel to others and urge them to repent. Today is truly the day of salvation.

Chapter 2

What will happen before Jesus comes back?

God has blessed my wife, Jennifer, and me with four children. They were all born naturally, and I was present throughout the entire process for each one. And to be completely honest, watching the birth of each of those children was simultaneously one of the most wonderful and most terrible experiences of my life.

It was wonderful, of course. Almost miraculous. How can I put into words the awe of seeing my own children born? Or of glimpsing the joy in my wife's eyes as she met each of her babies for the first time? How could I ever forget that sudden swell of fatherly devotion that filled my heart? Each birth was a sublime moment.

But in stark contrast, the labor leading up to each delivery was sheer horror. It involved hours and hours of screaming, moaning, sweating and crying. Was I in a maternity ward or a gulag? As the hours dragged on, the labor pains grew worse, and I couldn't do anything to help my wife besides offer feeble encouragement. I watched her writhe in pain through each successive, intensifying contraction.

Don't you feel sorry for me?

In the first chapter we saw that the world will end when Jesus returns as judge. For those who believe the gospel and no longer need to fear the wrath of the Lamb, Jesus' appearing at the end of the world will be like the moment a child is born: joyous, miraculous, sublime. When we see Jesus again, it will be the best day ever.

But before the miracle of birth comes the torment of labor. Before the rapturous joy comes the escalating agony. And that's how Jesus described the events leading up to his second coming. He called them "birth pains." What will happen before Jesus comes back? The world will go through labor.

> As Jesus was sitting on the Mount of Olives, the disciples came to him privately. "Tell us," they said, "when will this happen, and what will be the sign of your coming and of the end of the age?"
>
> Jesus answered: "Watch out that no one deceives you. For many will come in my name, claiming, 'I am the Messiah,' and will deceive many. You will hear of wars and rumors of wars, but see to it that you are not alarmed. Such things must happen, but the end is still to come. Nation

will rise against nation, and kingdom against kingdom. There will be famines and earthquakes in various places. All these are the beginning of birth pains.

"Then you will be handed over to be persecuted and put to death, and you will be hated by all nations because of me. At that time many will turn away from the faith and will betray and hate each other, and many false prophets will appear and deceive many people. Because of the increase of wickedness, the love of most will grow cold, but the one who stands firm to the end will be saved. And this gospel of the kingdom will be preached in the whole world as a testimony to all nations, and then the end will come."

Matthew 24 v 3-14

If the time before Jesus' return is like birth pains, then these verses are like a birthing class. They explain what the process prior to the birth will be like. When my wife was pregnant with our first child, we attended a birthing class together. The class covered the stages of labor, possible complications, and events to be expected, like water breaking and epidurals administered. We even watched a lovely, graphic video of actual labors and deliveries. The goal of the class was to give us realistic expectations of the birth event so we would be ready.

Similarly, that's what Jesus was doing in those verses. He was preparing his disciples to stand firm for him by setting their expectations about the future birth pains. He didn't say these things to frighten or confuse his followers. He tells us what to expect because he loves us and doesn't want us to be thrown off when things in the world seem difficult. A lot of difficult things lie ahead, and Jesus doesn't want us to panic when those things happen, or to mistakenly think that it is the end of the world when in reality the end may still be a long way off. So let's go through Jesus' labor lecture again and study in detail what will happen before he comes back so that we, too, might be prepared to stay true to Jesus, no matter what.

False messiahs and false prophets

The first words out of Jesus' mouth in these verses are: "Watch out that no one deceives you" (v 4). Jesus warns his followers that prior to his return, phony religious leaders will pop up and mislead people. These impostors will come in two varieties.

First, there are false Christs. Jesus tells us to beware of people who say: "I am the Messiah" (v 5). Down through the centuries different individuals have claimed to be some variation of the Messiah. In the 18th century, Ann Lee, one of the leaders of a religious group called the Shakers, proclaimed herself to be Jesus' female counterpart. And then there was Sun Myung Moon, the 20th-century Korean founder of the "Moonies," who said he was the second coming of Christ. These false Messiahs confused and deceived many. But Jesus has made it clear: if someone claims to be the Messiah, don't fall for it.

Second, Jesus raised the alarm about false prophets. These are people who claim to bring a direct message from God. Jesus cautioned that some fake prophets might even perform miraculous signs (v 24). But you can always spot a false prophet because he leads people astray from the Jesus of the Bible either by denying Jesus completely or, more often, by proclaiming some deformed version of Jesus that doesn't square with what the Bible teaches.

For example, we might think of Joseph Smith, the prophet who founded Mormonism. His Mormon doctrine teaches that Jesus is a procreated being, produced by the union of God the Father and a spirit wife. Further, Jesus was simply the first among many spirit children born to God into the world. Among Jesus' many siblings was Lucifer, the devil himself! Hundreds of millions of people still follow the words of these prophets today.

And what about all the gurus and teachers and experts who don't call themselves "messiahs" or "prophets" but who claim to have the secret for finding hope, prosperity and success (all for a substantial fee)?

Or even more common are those persuasive and confident "Bible teachers" who distort the Scriptures and create mini-followings in local churches. These false prophets pull people away from the gospel and get them focused on novel teachings, speculations and even supposed messages from the Holy Spirit.

Keep your eyes on Jesus and keep studying your Bible. That way, when a false prophet starts spouting off, you will be able to pick out the counterfeit message and avoid being led astray.

Who is the antichrist?

Question: *What did Nero, Charlemagne, Napoleon and Hitler all have in common, besides ruling nations?*

Answer: *They were all identified as being the antichrist!*

Throughout history, various individuals have been suspected of being the antichrist, that ultimate false Messiah who would be like Satan incarnate and would fool the world into worshiping and following him. And yet in every case, the candidate for the job of antichrist died and the world moved on.

So who is this antichrist and how will we identify him (or her)? The apostle John gave this surprising answer:

> Dear children, this is the last hour; and as you have heard that the antichrist is coming, even now many antichrists have come. This is how we know it is the last hour. They went out from us, but they did not really belong to us. For if they had belonged to us, they would have remained with us; but their going showed that none of them belonged to us. ... Who is the liar? It is whoever denies that Jesus is the Christ. Such a person is the antichrist—denying the Father and the Son.
> *1 John 2 v 18-19, 22*

Did you catch that? According to John, there are *many antichrists*. Furthermore, some had already arisen in his own time and had been part of his church! Who is the antichrist? It is "whoever denies that Jesus is the

Christ" (v 22). That makes sense: a person who denies that Jesus is the Christ is literally anti (against) Christ.

John said something similar in his second letter: "Many deceivers, who do not acknowledge Jesus Christ as coming in the flesh, have gone out into the world. Any such person is the deceiver and the antichrist." (2 John v 7). Apparently you don't have to rule an empire to qualify as an antichrist. You only have to deny that Jesus is the Messiah and that he came as a man to save us. It's no surprise that there have been so many candidates for antichrist down through the centuries, because so many have denied and opposed Jesus and the gospel. The spirit of antichrist is clearly at work in the world (see 1 John 4 v 3).

But what about the final antichrist? Will there be an ultimate, super Jesus-rejecter who will arise to mislead the world at the very end? It seems so. John did say: "you have heard that the antichrist is coming" (1 John 2 v 18). It appears that even though he saw many antichrists in his own day, he still acknowledged a final antichrist. And the apostle Paul taught about a future "man of lawlessness," a figure who "will oppose and will exalt himself over everything that is called God or is worshiped, so that he sets himself up in God's temple, proclaiming himself to be God." (2 Thessalonians 2 v 4). You can't get much more opposed to Jesus than that.

So be on the lookout for the antichrist. But don't focus primarily on presidents and prime ministers. Rather, listen carefully for those everyday voices, even voices in your own church, that deny Jesus and make him something less than the Son of God, the Messiah, and the Savior of the world.

Wars and disasters

Nothing makes it seem that the world is unraveling as much as war or natural disasters. And yet Jesus told his disciples to *expect* these things. Wars, famines and earthquakes would not be the end of the world; they are merely part of the birth pains that precede Jesus' return.

Jesus said, "Nation will rise against nation, and kingdom against kingdom" (Matthew 24 v 7). Was he ever right! War has raged ever since he spoke those words. Of course, there are many examples of positive, peaceful advances in human culture since the time of Christ. The last century saw amazing progress in medicine, technology and communication that has brought huge improvements to the lives of billions. In many ways our technological progress has improved human existence.

Yet even as the 20th century witnessed astounding achievements, it also saw some of that same technology employed to make it the bloodiest, war-torn, genocidal century in human history.

Are we even one step closer to world peace today? Jesus was right. Humanity has continued in its warlike ways.

Furthermore, "there will be famines and earthquakes in various places" (v 7). It's as if the physical world itself will experience the labor cramps before Jesus returns. Not surprisingly, when you read the book of Revelation, you find that many of the terrible visions of judgment involve just these sorts of things: wars, plagues, famines, earthquakes, and economic crashes. And as you move through the cycles of visions in Revelation, the judgments seem to increase in intensity... just like labor.

But here was Jesus' original point: when these kinds of dreadful calamities take place, don't mistakenly think the world is ending. No, "all these are the *beginning* of birth pains" (v 8).

Persecution

Jesus had an even bigger concern for his followers than wars and disasters. He wanted to make sure they weren't caught off guard by something else that was coming: persecution. Again, he said: "Then you will be handed over to be persecuted and put to death, and you will be hated by all nations because of me." (v 9).

His words proved true. Church tradition tells us that all of the disciples except John were martyred, and John spent his last days in exile for his faith. But it didn't stop with those guys. The disciples of the disciples endured abuse from the Roman emperors. They were crucified, burned, and served up as lunch for the lions.

Sadly, the persecution didn't stop there either. Christians continue to suffer and even die for their faith all around the world today. Those who track religious persecution tell us that more Christians were martyred in the 20th century than in all the previous centuries combined. As the gospel has spread, so has tribulation for gospel people.

Don't be surprised if persecution continues right up until Jesus returns. Interestingly, there are several places in the Bible that seem to describe the world at the very, very end, right before Jesus returns. And in them we find what seems to be a final war waged against God's people under the direction of a diabolical leader. It's as if Jesus must intervene in the end to save his followers from extinction. False messiahs, war, and persecution are not going away. They are the birth pains.

The Bible gives us these warnings so that we might not jump ship when persecution happens. "Hey God, I never signed up for this! I thought Jesus was supposed to solve my problems, not create new ones. Isn't Jesus supposed to bless his followers with health and prosperity?" Suffering tests our faith, revealing who's really committed to Jesus and who merely looks to him as a kind of heavenly Santa Claus. Jesus warned that many would fall away when persecution came (v 10).

But Jesus never promised that his followers would live large or escape hardship. Rather, he said: "Whoever wants to be my disciple must deny themselves and take up their cross daily and follow me" (Luke 9 v 23). Just as Jesus had to face the cross before receiving his crown, so his followers must be ready to endure persecution before Jesus returns to bring his kingdom in all its glory. As the apostle Paul told the Christians in his day: "We must go through many hardships to enter the kingdom of God" (Acts 14 v 22).

Wickedness and lawlessness

As if that list of labor pains wasn't bad enough, in Matthew 24 v 12 Jesus also mentions wickedness (translated in some Bibles as "lawlessness"). The world will continue its moral decay right up until the end.

We have already mentioned warfare. Consider the other moral evils that continue today. Narcotics devour the lives of untold numbers of people, and wreak havoc in families and communities. Human trafficking and the sex trade victimize tens of millions. People across the planet view pornography in the comfort of their home through the internet.

And then there's perhaps the most radical social evil of all: abortion. Abortion is the single greatest cause of death for human beings today. According to World Health Organization estimates, some 40 to 50 million babies are aborted in the world each year. That's over 100,000 babies per day. That's far more than die annually from heart disease, respiratory infections, strokes, and HIV/AIDS combined. The world has never before seen murder of this magnitude carried out. And if all this was not bad enough, each of these lawless trends— drugs, slavery, pornography and abortion—has become a massive multimillion or even multibillion-dollar industry.

But this rejection of God's laws doesn't only show up in the big, global atrocities. The lawlessness preceding Jesus' return expresses itself in everyday attitudes. Paul put it this way:

> But mark this: There will be terrible times in the last days. People will be lovers of themselves, lovers of money, boastful, proud, abusive, disobedient to their parents, ungrateful, unholy, without love, unforgiving, slanderous, without self-control, brutal, not lovers of the good, treacherous, rash, conceited, lovers of pleasure rather than lovers of God—having a form of godliness but

And did you notice that last phrase? "Having a form of
godliness" seems to indicate that this lawlessness will
even infect the Christian community.

To be clear, Jesus' words don't mean that everything
happening in the world today is negative and lawless.
By God's grace there are still good things taking place.
Nor should Christians respond to Jesus' teaching by
throwing up their hands in defeat, locking themselves
in an end-times bunker and no longer trying to make
the world a better place. Jesus doesn't call us to fiddle
while the world burns. Rather, Christians should pray
and strive for a better society. We should be active in
things like politics and medicine, social work and edu-
cation. We should still long to see God glorified even
in the midst of depravity, and we should still love our
neighbors and seek their good even when they want
nothing to do with God.

But make no mistake. We will have to contend with
lawlessness and sin in every culture right up until the
end. Jesus said so.

Gospel growth

Yes, things are bad in the world. The labor pains preceding birth are painful and distressing. But even during
labor something wonderful is happening. The baby is
on its way! And during the world's labor before Jesus returns, something else wonderful is happening: the gospel is spreading to all nations. At the end of the list of

labor pains Jesus says: "And this gospel of the kingdom will be preached in the whole world as a testimony to all nations, and then the end will come" (v 14).

Why must the gospel be preached to all nations? For at least two reasons: 1) the gospel warns all nations and kingdoms that Jesus is the true King and that he is coming back as the world's Judge; and 2) the gospel gathers in the citizens of Jesus' kingdom as people from all nations repent of their sins and trust in Jesus as their Savior. Once all the peoples are warned and all the citizens are assembled, the king will return.

Think about how that gospel message has in fact been spreading around the world. Jesus began by preaching to the Jews, and a small band of disciples believed. Those disciples traveled across the Roman Empire proclaiming the gospel, going west into Europe and as far east as India. Despite persecution and hostility, followers of Jesus multiplied around the Mediterranean region. Eventually the gospel spread throughout Europe, but it seemed to stall out there for several centuries for the most part.

Then in the late 18th century, the gospel made a fresh geographical surge through the labors of people like William Carey, the father of modern missions. Missionaries from North America and Europe took the good news of Jesus to people who had never heard his name. As a result of these missionary labors, Christianity's center of gravity today has shifted from North America and Europe to South America, Africa and Asia. And now those believers are sending out missionaries.

And yet there is still more to do. Clearly, now is not the time for us to retreat into a Christian compound, bar the doors, stockpile food, and glumly wait for the end. Now is the time to go out into the world with love, courage and joy as we tell our friends and neighbors the good news about Jesus. Now is the time to risk our lives and fortunes to go to people who have never heard about salvation through the cross and the empty tomb. The labor pains like wars or persecution should warn us against clinging to this world too tightly, and liberate us to live boldly for Jesus and speed his arrival.

Don't you see? It's all happening! Everything Jesus said is coming to pass, both the tribulations and the kingdom, both the increase of evil and the advance of the gospel. And we can live in confidence that this gospel will be preached to all nations. And then the end will come.

But how exactly will we know when that end has come? How will we know when the labor is over and the moment of birth is at hand? We turn to that question in the next chapter.

Are we in the end times yet?

A church member once asked me: "Do you think we're living in the end times?" My answered surprised her. I said: "Yes, we are definitely in the end times. In fact we have been in the end times for almost two thousand years now."

When Christians today use the phrase "end times" they often seem to be thinking of some relatively brief, future period immediately preceding the return of Jesus. But when we read the New Testament, we find that Christians back then saw the end times as something that began with the first coming of Jesus. They used a variety of terms to refer to the end times, like "last days," "culmination of the ages" and "final hour." But regardless of the phrase used, they clearly saw the end times as something that had already begun.

There are many New Testament examples of this understanding of the end times. Let's just look at a few verses. Notice that in each example the writer understood the end times as present in his own day. The end had already begun.

- **The apostle Paul:** "These things happened to them as examples and were written down as warnings for us, on whom **the culmination of the ages** has come" 1 Corinthians 10 v 11.

- **Author of Hebrews:** "In the past God spoke to our ancestors through the prophets at many times and in various ways, but **in these last days** he has spoken to us by his Son" Hebrews 1 v 1-2.

- **The apostle John:** "Dear children, this is **the last**

hour; and as you have heard that the antichrist is coming, so now many antichrists have come. Therefore we know it is the last hour" 1 John 2 v 18.

- **Jude, the brother of Jesus:** "'In **the last times** there will be scoffers who will follow their own ungodly desires.' These are the people who divide you, who follow mere natural instincts and do not have the Spirit" Jude v 18-19.

When the New Testament writers looked at their Old Testament Scriptures and saw prophecies about the latter days, they understood those prophecies as having begun to be fulfilled in Jesus and his church.

So does this mean that there are no end-times events still to come? Is there no future aspect to the last days? The imagery that Jesus gave us of labor and birth again helps us. Just as labor is a process that occurs over time with increasing intensity, so these last days are taking place over a lengthy period and are gradually escalating in magnitude. Or to put it another way, the end times have already begun but are not yet completed. That's why we saw in this chapter the many ways in which Jesus' words in Matthew 24 have already come to pass. And yet we can still expect further and larger fulfillments. That's why John could say that the antichrist is yet to come, but already many antichrists have come (see the section entitled: "Who is the antichrist?").

So when my friend asked: "Are we in the end times?," perhaps a more accurate question would have been: "Are we in the end of the end times yet?" Unfortunately, that's a question this pastor cannot answer.

Chapter 3

How will Jesus come back?

Throughout our lives we envision certain "big days" that we hope will come to pass. Girls sometimes dress up like brides and practice walking down the aisle, dreaming of their wedding day. Boys kick soccer balls in the park and fantasize about making the game-winning goal in the World Cup.

Even as adults we visualize watershed moments like when we finally get the diploma, open the business, buy the car, hold the newborn, cross the threshold of our first home, or leave work for the last time as we glide into retirement. Prisoners picture themselves finally walking out of the jail, and cancer patients dare to dream of an appointment when their oncologist says: "The treatment worked. You're in remission!"

But have you ever tried to imagine what it will be like

on the greatest day of all, the day when Jesus returns and the world ends?

Perhaps that day is too massive to visualize. Thinking about Jesus' return feels like trying to get your head around the concept of eternity or the doctrine of the Trinity. The thought of him coming back can overload our imagination circuits, as well as overwhelm our hearts. Peter said: "Though you have not seen him, you love him" (1 Peter 1 v 8). How much more will we love him when we finally see him face to face? Could it be that we aren't supposed to consider the day of Jesus' return because it is simply too big and too wonderful?

Yet Jesus himself invites us to picture that day. He gives glimpses in the Bible of the moment when he shows up and the world shuts down. Let's look at one of those sneak peeks at his second coming:

> Immediately after the distress of those days
> > "the sun will be darkened,
> > and the moon will not give its light;
> > the stars will fall from the sky,
> > and the heavenly bodies will be shaken."
> Then will appear the sign of the Son of Man in heaven. And then all the peoples of the earth will mourn when they see the Son of Man coming on the clouds of heaven, with power and great glory. And he will send his angels with a loud trumpet call, and they will gather his elect from the four winds, from one end of the heavens to the other.
> *Matthew 24 v 29-31*

What will it be like when Jesus returns? We won't know fully until that day arrives. But based on this snapshot of the end, and others like it in the Bible, there are several things we can say about the last day. We know that Jesus will return publicly, gloriously, victoriously and savingly.

Publicly

When Jesus comes back, everyone will know it.

It won't be like his first appearance when he slipped quietly into the world as the baby in Bethlehem's manger. None of the world's rulers realized the King of kings had arrived on that first Christmas morning. The only people who knew the Savior was born were some shepherds, a few astrologers (the "wise men"), and of course the newly-wed peasants, Joseph and Mary—hardly a fitting welcoming committee for the Messiah.

But at the end of the world, at Christmas the sequel, Jesus will return publicly and visibly. His arrival will be globally experienced. Nobody will wake up the day after Jesus' return wondering what everyone else is talking about. "What? Jesus came back? I must have been surfing the internet and missed him. Did anyone get a video of it?"

Notice how our verse describes a public, visible, unmistakable second coming.

- The sun and moon will be darkened and stars will "fall".

- The sign of the "Son of Man" (Jesus' name for

himself, taken from Daniel 7) will appear in the sky.

- All people will see Jesus coming on the clouds of heaven and they will mourn.

- The trumpet will sound and angels will go out to gather God's people.

In fact, just before our passage, Jesus emphatically warned his disciples against believing false reports of his return precisely because his return would be so universally obvious.

> So if anyone tells you, "There he is, out in the wilderness," do not go out; or, "Here he is, in the inner rooms," do not believe it. For as lightning that comes from the east is visible even in the west, so will be the coming of the Son of Man.
>
> *Matthew 24 v 26-27*

Jesus' return will command the largest audience of any event in human history. Like lightning flashing, it will be visible from one end of the sky to the other. You won't be able to miss it even if you try.

Will there be a secret rapture?

Many Christians today believe that Jesus' second coming will happen in phases. According to this view, Jesus will first come unexpectedly and invisibly in order to gather believers out of the world, and then come again later in the visible, awesome way described here in Matthew 24. This prior coming is sometimes called the "secret rapture." It's secret because the world won't see Jesus at this event and won't have any warning of his coming. And it's a "rapture," which means that Christians will be "caught up" out of this world to be with Jesus. However, we should remember that "rapture" is not a word found in the Bible.

At the secret rapture, all the Christians will mysteriously vanish from the world and those who are left behind will suffer the terrible judgments and tribulations described in the book of Revelation. The period between the secret rapture and the visible return of Jesus is often referred to in this view as "the tribulation."

The "secret rapture" theory was first made popular in the late 19th century by a Bible teacher named John Nelson Darby, and spread widely through the Scofield Reference Bible. It is part of a larger theological school known as "Dispensationalism." Many Christians are familiar with this view today through books like *Left Behind*.

Will there be a secret rapture prior to Jesus' public return? Perhaps we should start by affirming that the Bible clearly teaches a rapture. Paul put it this way:

> **For the Lord himself will come down from heaven, with a loud command, with the voice of the archangel and with the trumpet call of God, and the dead in Christ will rise first. After that, we who are still alive and are left will be caught up together with them in the clouds to meet the Lord in the air. And so we will be with the Lord forever. Therefore encourage one another with these words.**
> *1 Thessalonians 4 v 16-17*

Jesus will gather his people by "rapturing" them up to himself. All Bible-believing Christians should be able to agree on and celebrate this truth!

But the question remains: will that rapture happen prior to Jesus' visible second coming? The challenge for this "left behind" scenario is that there isn't a biblical text that clearly teaches a secret rapture as an event distinct from the second coming. Bible verses supposedly teaching the secret rapture could also be read as depicting Jesus' public return. For example, the text we just read from 1 Thessalonians 4 v 16-17 describes a seemingly public return of Jesus similar in many respects to what we've been reading about in Matthew 24. In both texts we have Jesus returning, trumpets blasting, angels mentioned, and believers gathered up. While it is theoretically possible that 1 Thessalonians 4 and Matthew 24 describe separate events, isn't it more natural to read them as both depicting the same global, visible return of Jesus, although with slightly different language? If you had never heard of the "secret rapture" theory, would a plain reading of 1 Thessalonians 4 v 16-17 lead you to think: "This must be a different event from the visible return of Jesus"?

Regardless of our view of the rapture, we need to keep this issue in perspective. The rapture should not be an issue that divides Christians or churches. One's rapture theory isn't an essential Christian doctrine like the Trinity or the resurrection of Jesus.

If you're a Christian who remains unconvinced by the "secret rapture" teaching, will you be upset if you're wrong and you get secretly raptured? "Sorry Jesus, but I don't want to you to take me prior to your second coming until you prove the 'secret rapture' theory from the Bible." On the other hand, if you do believe in the secret rapture, will you stop faithfully following Jesus if the secret rapture doesn't happen?

Gloriously

Jesus' return won't just be global; it will also be gloriously. It will shine and burn and shake the universe to its foundations. His appearing will cause wonder and wailing, awe and dread, rejoicing and writhing. Everyone will see it, and everyone will be blown away—in one way or another. Jesus said: "Then all the peoples of the earth will mourn when they see the Son of Man coming on the clouds of heaven, with power and great glory" (Matthew 24 v 30). At his majestic appearing the "sign of the Son of Man" will appear in the sky. Many commentators see the "sign" as referring to a banner or ensign. When the King makes his global debut, the trumpets will blast and his flag will wave gloriously.

Again, compare his second coming to his first. It was as if Jesus went to great lengths to hide that glory the first time he came. He was born in the backwaters of the Roman Empire and grew up as a carpenter's son in an insignificant town.

During his public ministry, many had a hard time believing he was the glorious "Son of Man." He traveled about like a wandering rabbi, not a conquering king. When he performed miracles, he often commanded people to keep it a secret. When he let his glory shine out for a moment at the transfiguration (check out Matthew 17 v 1-9), he ordered the disciples with him not to tell anyone about it until after his resurrection. His life reached its crescendo in a moment of ultimate shame and degradation: his crucifixion. To be sure, the glory of God's power, mercy and goodness blazed in Jesus' life and death, but it took spiritual x-ray vision to see it.

It won't take spiritual super-powers to see his imperial glory when he comes the second time. Jesus' kingly authority, his divine power and his brilliant holiness will cause the creation to come unhinged and all people to be undone.

Victoriously

We can go a step further. Jesus's return will be more than glorious; it will be utterly triumphant. Jesus will come as conquering King to overthrow all his enemies. That's why when he returns "all the peoples of the earth will mourn" (Matthew 24 v 30). On that day, the opportunity to hear and receive the gospel will end and humanity will be forced to face the Lord they have rejected again and again.

The defeat and overthrow of an unbelieving world is also signaled by a cosmic meltdown: sun and moon no longer shine, and the heavenly bodies are shaken. We already saw in chapter 1 that the Bible often uses this sort of heavenly "de-creation" imagery to describe what it will be like on the Day of the Lord, when God brings judgment on his enemies.

Revelation 19 gives perhaps the Bible's strongest, most awe-inspiring depiction of Jesus' coming in victory and judgment over the world:

I saw heaven standing open and there before me was a white horse, whose rider is called Faithful and True. With justice he judges and wages war. His eyes are like blazing fire, and on his head are many crowns. He has a name written on him that no one knows but he himself. He is dressed in a robe dipped in blood, and his name is the Word of God. The armies of heaven were following him, riding on white horses and dressed in fine linen, white and clean. Coming out of his mouth is a sharp sword with which to strike down the nations. "He will rule them with an iron scepter." He treads the winepress of the fury of the wrath of God Almighty. On his robe and on his thigh he has this name written: KING OF KINGS AND LORD OF LORDS. *Revelation 19 v 11-16*

What happens when Jesus returns at the end of the world? All the forces in heaven and on earth that refuse Jesus as the King of kings and Lord of lords will be confronted and put down. All of the unbelief and indifference, disobedience and wickedness in the cosmos will give way to grieving and dread when Jesus appears as conquering Judge. Imagine living your entire life tuning out God's word, breaking God's laws, and refusing God's Son, Jesus, as Savior and Lord; and then suddenly seeing that everything you disbelieved and rejected is terrifyingly true. The Father will fully vindicate his Son, to the dismay of an unbelieving world.

Savingly

Not everyone will mourn on that day when Jesus returns publicly and gloriously. Some will have reason to rejoice as never before. On the day the world ends, Jesus will send out his angels "and they will gather his elect from the four winds, from one end of the heavens to the other" (Matthew 24 v 31). Jesus will return savingly for his people.

In fact, Matthew records several instances in which Jesus spoke about his return and about sending out his angels to collect and save his people. He said that final-day gathering would be like:

- **a farmer** who gathers both wheat and weeds, storing the wheat in the barn and burning the weeds (Matthew 13 v 24-30)

- **a fisherman** who gathers fish in his nets, putting the good fish into containers and throwing out the worthless ones (Matthew 13 v 47-52)

- **a shepherd** who gathers his flocks before him, separating the sheep from the goats (Matthew 25 v 31-46).

Listen to what Jesus will say to his elect sheep on that day: "Come, you who are blessed by my Father; take your inheritance, the kingdom prepared for you since the creation of the world" (Matthew 25 v 34). At long last we will inherit the kingdom of God in all of its fulness.

Can you imagine that moment?

Just think about it. You have lived your entire Christian life in this sinful and broken world. Throughout your pilgrimage you have walked by faith, not by sight. You have trusted that God has a plan but often didn't know what that plan could possibly be. Yes, you have known Jesus. But even your closest fellowship with him has been fleeting, limited, and invisible. Sometimes you wondered if he was there at all. And sometimes you wondered if you were a Christian at all, given how your obedience to Jesus and love for him rose and fell like the ocean tide.

On the one hand, you have been saved from the penalty of sin by Jesus' death and resurrection, and you are now being saved from the power of sin by the Holy Spirit. On the other hand, you continue to discover new pockets of sin in your heart, and the struggle to follow Jesus continues. Though you are a child of the King, you have lived your whole life as a stranger and alien in this world, at times mocked and mistreated because of your faith in Jesus.

But when Jesus comes again, all of that will change forever. Jesus will gather you to himself. At long last your fleeting fellowship with Christ will give way to direct contact as you see him face to face. You will go from being a refugee in the world to being a ruler with Christ. You will no longer be like Abraham and his family, camping out as strangers in the promised land. Instead you will be like the Israelites triumphantly following Joshua across the Jordan into your inheritance. When Jesus returns, you will be saved to sin no more, to grieve no more, to die no more. For those who love Jesus, the end of the world will bring the fulfillment of all hope.

The last day will be our best day.

Chapter 4

Will Jesus come back before or after the "Millennium"?

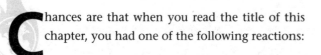

hances are that when you read the title of this chapter, you had one of the following reactions:

- Reaction #1: "Finally! I was wondering when we were going to get to the good stuff."

- Reaction #2: "I can feel myself getting confused already."

- Reaction #3: "Who cares? I'm just glad Jesus is coming back."

To everyone who had the first reaction: yes, this chapter will include timelines and discussions of things like the "millennium" and "the tribulation." But remember, I didn't intend this book to provide an in-depth analysis of various end-times schemes. Rather, the book seeks to point us back to the primary focus of the New Testament's teaching about the end of the world, namely that Jesus is returning.

If you had the second reaction, then you've come to the right chapter. The New Testament teaching about things like the end of the world, the millennium and the final judgment can feel a bit like a jigsaw puzzle. It's not surprising that over the centuries Christians have created different ways of putting the puzzle pieces together. In this chapter we will try to get our heads around the different ways in which people have tried to make sense of the biblical data, and to understand each view's strengths and weaknesses.

Those who had the third reaction may be tempted to skip this part entirely. But please keep reading. Even if you're like me and you don't hold the millennium to be a Bible doctrine essential to our salvation, there's something to be gained through digging into the topic. By studying the relationship of Jesus' return to the millennium, we find ourselves starting to put the end-times pieces together, one way or another. It helps us to connect the dots of the Bible's teaching about the end of the world, and to understand why other Christians read parts of the Bible in the way they do. Having a sense of how the whole fits together, or could fit together, enables us to make sense of the details.

But first things first. What is this "millennium?"

The thousand-year reign

A "millennium" is a 1,000-year period. In Christian theology, the millennium refers to the 1,000-year period described in Revelation 20 v 1-6.

> And I saw an angel coming down out of heaven, having the key to the Abyss and holding in his hand a great chain. He seized the dragon, that ancient serpent, who is the devil, or Satan, and bound him for a thousand years. He threw him into the Abyss, and locked and sealed it over him, to keep him from deceiving the nations anymore until the thousand years were ended. After that, he must be set free for a short time.
>
> I saw thrones on which were seated those who had been given authority to judge. And I saw the souls of those who had been beheaded because of their testimony about Jesus and because of the word of God. They had not worshiped the beast or its image and had not received its mark on their foreheads or their hands. They came to life and reigned with Christ a thousand years. (The rest of the dead did not come to life until the thousand years were ended.) This is the first resurrection. Blessed and holy are those who share in the first resurrection. The second death has no power over them, but they will be priests of God and of Christ and will reign with him for a thousand years. *Revelation 20 v 1-6*

This is the only place in the Bible that we find an explicit reference to this 1,000 year period. Nonetheless, the text is remarkable. An angel imprisons Satan, and

Jesus raises and enthrones his martyrs for a millennium. It sounds wonderfully epic, doesn't it?

The passage also raises all kinds of questions. Is this a literal 1,000 years? Do all Christians come to life during the millennium, or only the martyrs, or only martyrs who died by beheading? Where exactly is "the Abyss"? What "nations" will be around during the millennium?

But let us start with a more basic question: *when does this millennium take place?* Is this something that has already happened, is happening, or is yet to happen? Or to connect the timing of the millennium to the return of Jesus, we might ask the question this way: *will Jesus return before or after the millennium of Revelation 20?*

When we ask whether Jesus returns before or after the millennium, there are two obvious ways in which people can answer the question.

Answer #1: Jesus will return before the millennium

This first way in which people answer the question is called "pre-millennialism." According to this view, Jesus returns before, or "pre," the millennium of Revelation 20 v 1-6. This way of reading the Bible sees Revelation 20 as describing something that hasn't happened yet and won't happen until after Jesus comes back. So you could say that in a pre-millennial reading, the end of the world begins when Jesus returns, but that the final end of the world comes 1,000 years after Christ's second coming.

Here are some of the more important arguments for the pre-millennial position:

- The millennium in Revelation 20 follows a vision of the return of Jesus in chapter 19.

- Satan seems contained during the millennium, unlike now when he seems highly active.

- The dead are resurrected to reign with Jesus during the millennium, something that doesn't appear to have happened yet.

- The millennium in Revelation 20 could be the fulfillment of many of the Old Testament prophecies about a seemingly "golden age" of God's reign on earth.

Perhaps the most compelling aspect of pre-millennialism is that it attempts to take Revelation 20 at face value. Jesus returns (Revelation 19), and then things happen that do not appear to have happened yet, like the devil's imprisonment, and the resurrection and reign of deceased Christians (chapter 20). It's not surprising, therefore, that many Christians read the Bible in a pre-millennial way.

But we need to go a step further. You should also know that pre-millennialists usually fall into one of two general schools. This animal we call "pre-millennialism" comes in two species.

Classic pre-millennialism
The first species or school of pre-millennialism is typically called "classic pre-millennialism." It's fairly straightforward. Classic pre-millennialism teaches that this cur-

rent age will continue with its trials and tribulations, as well as with the advance of the gospel. At the end of this age, Jesus will return. Satan will be bound, and believers (either all or a portion of them) will be resurrected and will reign on earth with Jesus for 1,000 years in a great golden era. At the end of the millennium, Satan will be released and will rebel, Jesus will defeat him, and then the final resurrection, the final judgment and the new creation will come (see next chapter for more on those final events).

Perhaps it's helpful to visualize this position:

CLASSIC PRE-MILLENNIALISM

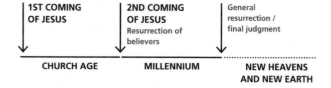

1ST COMING OF JESUS	2ND COMING OF JESUS Resurrection of believers	General resurrection / final judgment
CHURCH AGE	MILLENNIUM	NEW HEAVENS AND NEW EARTH

Classic pre-millennialists may differ on some of the details, like what events lead up to Jesus' return, or whether the millennium is a literal 1,000 years or whether "1,000" symbolizes a very long period of time. But they all agree that the millennium will occur after Jesus returns. Classic pre-millennialism, or at least a certain version of it, was the first end-times scheme to appear in the writings of church history.

Dispensational pre-millennialism

There is a second type of pre-millennialism usually called

"dispensationalism." While classic pre-millennialism is the oldest-known system, dispensationalism is the newest. Modern dispensationalism was first articulated in the late 19th century and spread quickly throughout North America and in many other parts of the world through the 20th century. It was popularized through the *Scofield Reference Bible* and books like *The Late Great Planet Earth* and the *Left Behind* series. Since then, this view has become perhaps the dominant, default way of putting together the Bible's end-of-the-world teachings. When many Christians think about the end of the world, they do so in dispensational categories without even realizing it.

To understand dispensationalism, we need first to appreciate its driving concern to read the Bible at face value and as a historical document. This belief strives to interpret the Bible plainly and literally, and resists attempts to "spiritualize" the Bible's stories and prophecies. As a result, dispensationalists tend to expect that the Old Testament promises and prophecies about Israel will be literally and historically fulfilled. Historically, dispensationalists have spoken of God's plans to save two distinct groups: Israel and the church. This belief then maps out how God works uniquely in different eras (or "dispensations") to save these two distinct people groups.

Many interpreters from the other schools of thought believe that God still has plans to save Israel, in the sense that God will bring many Jewish people to believe in Jesus and join the church. But historic dispensationalism hopes for something more: a literal re-establishment of Israel as a nation ruled directly by God in the literal promised land, enjoying the blessings promised in Old Testament prophecies.

Here's the general sequence of events in a dispensational interpretation, or at least dispensationalism in its more well-known form.

- God made promises and prophecies to Israel in the Old Testament. He would bless them, give them authority over the nations, establish them in the promised land, and more.

- Israel failed to obey God's law again and again. They even rejected Jesus, God's Messiah (anointed King) for Israel.

- God turned away from Israel for a time and began his plan to save the Gentiles. In this new dispensation, sometimes called the "church age," God has put his plans for Israel on hold while he saves Gentiles through the gospel.

- At the end of the church's dispensation, God will re-initiate his plans to save Israel. To do that, God must first take the church out of the picture. This removal is the "secret rapture" of the church (see chapter 3). Interestingly, many dispensationalists believe that the rapture will happen soon because Israel became a nation again in 1948, signaling that God was about to resume his plan for Israel.

- After the rapture, God will unleash the terrible prophecies of judgment and woe described in

Revelation as occurring over a seven-year period, often called "the great tribulation." By the way, this is also why dispensationalism is sometimes called "pre-tribulational pre-millennialism." Jesus will supposedly rapture the church before, or pre, the tribulation.

■ God will also bring Jews to believe in Jesus during the tribulation.

■ At the end of the tribulation, Jesus will return to judge the world and begin his millennial reign on earth with Israel. It is during this 1,000-year period that many of the Old Testament's grand promises and prophecies to Israel will be fulfilled.

Again, it might be helpful to see a timeline:

DISPENSATIONAL PRE-MILLENNIALISM

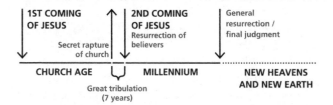

Dispensationalism is surely the most complex and comprehensive scheme for putting together the Bible's teachings about the end of the world. This short description barely scratches the surface of the dispensational model. And we haven't addressed the different ways that dispensational thought has changed over the past years.

But here's the bottom line: if you overhear people in an end-of-the-world conversation talking about events in the Middle East related to the present nation of Israel, the coming one-world government, the secret rapture, the tribulation, or expectations that we are in the final generation, there's a good chance those folks are reading the Bible through a dispensational lens, whether they realize it or not.

Answer #2: Jesus will return after the millennium

There is a second way to answer the question: *will Jesus return before or after the millennium?* While some read Revelation 20 and see an obvious description of a future event, others see it as something that is currently taking place, or will take place before Jesus returns. This view is commonly called "post-millennialism," because it teaches that Jesus will return after, or "post," the millennium of Revelation 20.

Here are a few of the arguments that lead many to a post-millennial reading:

- Post-millennialists emphasize what they see as the highly symbolic character of Revelation, and of apocalyptic writings in general, and so they don't immediately assume Revelation 20 describes a literal 1,000 years, a literal Abyss and chain for Satan, or even that the "first resurrection" of Revelation 20 is a literally physical resurrection, any more than the "second death" (Revelation 20 v 6) is a literally physical death in the way we commonly talk about death.

▦ The release of Satan and his final defeat at the end of the "millennium" (see Revelation 20 v 7-8) has significant similarities to the description of Jesus' victorious return in Revelation 19, signaling that Revelation 19 and 20 may depict the same event with different imagery, rather than two consecutive events.

▦ Satan's imprisonment is not necessarily a total removal of his work in the world, but is specifically interpreted within the text as him not being able to "[deceive] the nations" (20 v 3).

If one of the most persuasive aspects of pre-millennialism is its seemingly face-value reading of Revelation 20, then we might argue that the most compelling argument for post-millennialism is that it seems to fit better with a plain reading of the New Testament. When we read the rest of the New Testament's teachings about the end of the world, and especially Jesus' own words, it seems rather simple: Jesus will return as Judge, and the dead will be raised and consigned either to eternal life or to eternal judgment. The New Testament nowhere else describes a millennial period after Jesus' return.

So then, from a post-millennial perspective, what is the millennium? The answer depends on which post-millennialist you ask. Post-millennialism comes in two species, just like pre-millennialism does.

Amillennialism

The first type of post-millennialism is usually called "amillennialism." It's most famous early supporter was Augustine of Hippo (354-430 AD). The label "amillennial" is somewhat misleading because the word literally means "no millennium." However, amillennialists do believe in the 1,000 years of Revelation 20. They just believe that the number 1,000 is a symbolic number, like most numbers in Revelation, and that it merely represents a long period of time. In addition, they believe that Revelation 20 describes the current church age, from a specific perspective and with particular emphasis.

The timeline from an amillennial perspective is very simple:

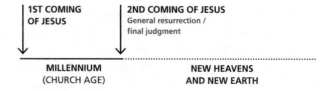

AMILLENNIALISM

| 1ST COMING OF JESUS | 2ND COMING OF JESUS
General resurrection /
final judgment |

| MILLENNIUM
(CHURCH AGE) | NEW HEAVENS
AND NEW EARTH |

In what way then does Revelation 20 describe the current church age? Amillennialism reads Revelation 20 as a symbolic description of the current spiritual victory that believers share with Christ.

The churches to whom Revelation was written faced persecution from without and deceivers from within. Even John, who wrote Revelation, did so from an island where he was exiled for his faith. Like us today, those

Christians could have looked at their circumstances and doubted that Jesus really reigned as King of kings and Lord of lords.

But in the amillennial understanding, Revelation 20 lifts the curtain to show us the spiritual realm. There we see that Satan has already been overcome, and as a result the gospel is going to the nations, whereas before Jesus was born, the nations had been deceived by Satan and so lived in spiritual darkness. Furthermore, believers have already begun to share in Jesus' resurrection and dominion now. The "first resurrection" (Revelation 20 v 5) either refers to believers experiencing new life at their conversion, or, more likely, at their death. Christians losing their life for their faith might seem defeated by the world, but in fact they enjoy life with Jesus in heaven. Revelation 20 shouts to a suffering church: "The martyrs are currently victors, not losers. So don't give up! Stand firm for Christ even at the cost of your life!"

Classic post-millennialism

A second version of post-millennialism is commonly known as, well, post-millennialism. For the sake of clarity, I will call this species "classic post-millennialism."

Classic post-millennialism sees the 1,000 years of Revelation 20 as a golden age of blessing on earth that will result from the spread of the gospel and its influence on the world before Jesus returns. As the gospel goes to the whole world, people will be saved and cultures will be impacted to such an extent that God's kingdom will be felt here on earth before the end. Post-millennialists often point to Jesus' parables about the global spread of the gospel as evidence.

Or to put it another way, classic post-millennialism agrees with amillennialism that Revelation 20 is a symbolic description of something that happens before Christ's return. But it disagrees with amillennialism in that it sees the millennium as something still future, and not as something describing the entire church-age.

Here's how we might diagram this view:

CLASSIC POST-MILLENNIALISM

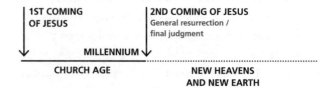

We might say that among the various end-times views, classic post-millennialism is the optimist. It anticipates the gospel advancing and transforming society. Classic post-millennialism held sway in the United States and Britain during the 18th and 19th centuries. This view was bolstered by the tremendous progress in technology, medicine and science, as well as by the emerging missionary movement. Not surprisingly, Christians at that time fueled social-reform movements like abolitionism. These Christians weren't merely trying to improve society. They hoped to usher in the millennium through their labors.

Classic post-millennialism doesn't have many vocal

supporters today. The 20th century saw two world wars, horrific genocides, global terrorism and more that have shattered the hopes of many that we might be on the verge of a worldwide peace.

Clear as mud? Did you figure it out? Have you decided if you are pre-millennial or post-millennial? Have the puzzle pieces fallen into place now?

It's probably too much to hope that this chapter would clear up all the questions. But I do hope it did at least three things:

1. I trust this chapter lifted you above the trees to see the forest. You now have categories that you can use to make some sense of end-times texts or conversations. You have "boxes" into which you can place the array of arguments and statements that people make about the end.

2. I pray this section increased your humility and patience toward others with different views. I firmly believe that millennial views should not divide Christians, and a better understanding of other views will help us guard against a dismissive, divisive attitude.

3. I hope this chapter increased your appetite to learn more about God's word. Rather than shying away from the parts of the Bible that talk about the end of the world, you now have some tools to dig deeper.

As your mind works to make sense of the details, may your heart swell with excitement that our Lord is returning!

How should we interpret the book of Revelation?

Bible-loving Christians struggle over how to piece together the end-of-the-world puzzle. To make matters worse, one of the major pieces to that puzzle is the book of Revelation, which is a puzzle in itself!

Revelation simultaneously fascinates us and befuddles us. It raises all kinds of questions. Should we interpret Revelation's strange visions more symbolically or more literally? Does Revelation describe past, present or future events? Do the visions in Revelation follow a chronological order, or are they at times cyclical and repetitive?

These questions go far beyond the scope of this book. But at the very least we can map out the four major approaches that people take to reading Revelation.

Preterism

Preterism sees Revelation primarily as a symbolic description of events in the first century. For example, the great beast out of the sea (chapter 13) is typically interpreted as Rome and one of its anti-Christian emperors like Nero (AD 37-68) or Domitian (AD 51-96). The great judgments and tribulations in Revelation describe God's wrath poured out either on Jerusalem in AD 70, or possibly the Roman empire. Preterists point to Matthew 24 (see also Mark 13 and Luke 21), where Jesus directly linked end-times events to the fall of Jerusalem. A major problem for Preterism is that it tends to take seemingly global descriptions of God's judgment and compress them into limited historical events, like the fall of Jerusalem.

Historicism

This interpretation views Revelation as a symbolic timeline of world history from Jesus' first coming to his second coming. The historicist tries to match up visions in Revelation with major events in world history. For example, some of the Protestant Reformers took a historicist approach and identified the pope as the antichrist. Others have interpreted the seven letters to the churches (Revelation 2 – 3) as a timeline of different stages in church history. A big hurdle for historicism is that it's fairly subjective: it turns Revelation into a historical ink-blot test. How do we know which world events are the ones being described by a particular vision in Revelation?

Futurism

Futurists interprets Revelation as mostly describing events that haven't happened yet. This approach typically reads Revelation as prophecy of the very end, just before Jesus returns. Futurism is akin to historicism, except that futurism believes Revelation relates primarily to the final slice of history. Futurism faces the challenge of showing how Revelation would have had any relevance for the first-century Christians to whom it was explicitly written.

Idealism

This approach doesn't attempt to tie Revelation's visions to specific historical events. Rather, it reads Revelation as a highly symbolic description of the spiritual conflict between Jesus and Satan, and good and evil, throughout history. Because idealism detaches Revelation from history, it also detaches us from a hope that Jesus will actually return to close history.

And one more...

There is one more approach to Revelation. You may have thought of it while you were reading this. In his commentary on Revelation, Greg Beale called this approach "**eclecticism**."[1] The view sees some truth in each of the other four views and tries to synthesize them somehow.

Over the years I have adopted an eclectic approach. I tend to read Revelation as describing spiritual realities that cycle throughout the church age. And yet those realities have concrete historical fulfillments, in the past, present and future. So for example, take again the "beast" of Revelation 13. When John wrote Revelation, that beast seems undoubtedly to have been Rome. But the beast didn't fall with the Roman Empire. It continues to rear its ugly, Christ-denying, church-devouring head in various world powers throughout church history. And I fear there will be a final, uber-beast at the very end, just before Jesus returns and the world ends.

Does that make me an idealist or a historicist? A preterist or a futurist? I'm not sure. But I do know this: it makes me a man who longs for the day when the shout will erupt: "The kingdom of the world has become the kingdom of our Lord and of his Messiah, and he will reign for ever and ever" (Revelation 11 v 15).

---

1 G.K. Beale, The New International Greek Testament Commentary: The Book of Revelation, Eerdemans, 2013.

Chapter 5

What happens after Jesus comes back?

Yes, there's more.

It might seem strange to ask: *what happens after Jesus comes back?* If the world ends when Jesus returns, how can there be an "after"? Isn't it game over and lights out for the human story?

Yet the Bible reveals that great, climactic events will unfold after Christ's second coming, events even greater than the millennium (see chapter 4). What happens after Jesus returns will dwarf everything that has come before it. Just as the end of classes and graduation mark the beginning of a student's journey in life, so too this world's finale is merely the beginning of our eternal saga. The end of the world is not the end of the story.

Revelation 20 v 11-15 provides a sobering preview of the world's epilogue:

Then I saw a great white throne and him who was seated on it. The earth and the heavens fled from his presence, and there was no place for them. And I saw the dead, great and small, standing before the throne, and books were opened. Another book was opened, which is the book of life. The dead were judged according to what they had done as recorded in the books. The sea gave up the dead that were in it, and death and Hades gave up the dead that were in them, and each person was judged according to what they had done. Then death and Hades were thrown into the lake of fire. The lake of fire is the second death. Anyone whose name was not found written in the book of life was thrown into the lake of fire.

This passage focuses our attention on four successive scenes, each of which tells us something about what will happen after Jesus comes back.

The great white throne

At the center of this vision, and of the entire book of Revelation for that matter, stands a great throne. This is God's throne. God rules all creation from his throne, and at the end he will judge humanity from that same throne. The prophet Daniel had a similar vision of the end: "As I looked, thrones were set in place, and the Ancient of Days took his seat. His clothing was as white as snow; the hair of his head was white like wool" (Daniel 7 v 9).

God's great white throne, standing at the end of history, should both comfort us and caution us. It comforts us because it promises that everything and everyone will answer to God. In our world, people get away with terrible evils. Genocide, war, slavery and corruption disfigure the human story. In the face of all this unanswered injustice, we cry out: "Where is God?"

God is where he has always been: on his throne. And that throne will have the final word. No one will get away with anything. In the end, justice and righteousness will prevail and every single sin will be accounted for. Be comforted!

And be cautioned: you and I are also part of this sinful and broken world that must answer to God.

The standing dead

Having confronted us with a staggering vision of God's throne, Revelation 20 zooms out to reveal a vast throng of people standing before the throne of God; a throng of dead people: "And I saw the dead, great and small, standing before the throne" (v 12). Death, Hades and the sea will all cough up their dead (v 13). Everyone will be present. We won't be able to hide from the great white throne. Not even the grave can conceal us. The earth and sky will flee from God's presence (v 11), but we won't have that option.

This vision of the dead standing before God reminds us that there will be a great resurrection of all people after Jesus comes back, though not all will be resurrected for the same destiny. We will appear before the throne of God in new bodies. Daniel prophesied: "Multitudes who sleep in the dust of the earth will awake: some to everlasting life, others to shame and everlasting contempt" (Daniel 12 v 2). And Jesus said: "Do not be amazed at this, for a time is coming when all who are in their graves will hear his voice and come out—those who have done what is good will rise to live, and those who have done what is evil will rise to be condemned" (John 5 v 28-29).

This final resurrection may come as a surprise because many people have a different vision of the afterlife, if they believe in an afterlife at all. You've probably heard this other version: when you die, you hover above your body for a bit, then travel up through a tunnel of blinding light. At the other end, deceased family members and friends await you. And so begins an eternal, ethereal, very well-lit family reunion.

Whatever our experience may be like when our souls leave our bodies, the fact is that experience will be temporary. God will resurrect all humanity from all the ages and summon them before his throne for a final reckoning, not a family picnic.

Books and the book

When the judge is seated and the defendants are standing, the trial will begin with a presentation of the evidence. The court will bring forward two documents. "Books were opened. Another book was opened, which is the book of life" (Revelation 20 v 12).

What exactly are these two pieces of evidence, these "books" and the "book of life?"

The "books" appear to be a record of each person's deeds, and serve as the basis for God's judgment: "The dead were judged according to what they had done as recorded in the books" (v 12). Imagine all your thoughts, words and deeds recorded and recounted before God!

The record books might surprise us, just as the resurrection does. Many people have a different expectation about how God will assess us on the judgment day. People sometimes imagine God judging us with a pair of scales rather than with account books. On one side of the scales God piles up our good deeds, and on the other side of the scales God piles up our bad deeds. And if your good acts outweigh your bad, if you're generally more kind than mean, if you're at least 51% decent, then you pass the test and go to heaven or paradise or some "better place."

But courtrooms don't use scales, and neither will the final court. Judges don't weigh good deeds against bad deeds in determining the defendant's guilt or innocence. An accused thief would never say to a judge: "Your Honor, I did indeed rob that bank at gunpoint. However, I have volunteered for several months at a homeless shelter. So taken on the whole, I'm a good person and don't deserve any punishment." The judge would slam down his gavel and say: "By your own admission you are guilty!"

Instead, judges and juries try to determine one thing: did the accused person break the law? And on that final day, the holy Judge of the universe will open the record of our lives to see if we have we violated his holy law. Have we broken his commandments? Have we lied, cheated, gossiped, coveted, sworn, stolen, lusted or blasphemed? Have we been sexually immoral, idolatrous, drunk, high, irreverent, unloving, unkind, enraged, violent, divisive, manipulative, arrogant, or dishonest? Have we ever failed to live out what Jesus said are the two greatest commandments in the Bible, namely to love God with all our hearts and to love our neighbors as ourselves?

How will you fare when the evidence of your entire life is measured against God's laws? Will you have a spotless record, or will there be ample evidence to prove you are a law-breaker?

The answer should be obvious: nobody will pass the test based on their deeds as recorded in the "books." All will be found as law-breakers. Therefore, there is only one hope of passing the final judgment. We must be recorded in the second document, the "book of life." Revelation 20 tells us that "anyone whose name was not found written in the book of life was thrown into the lake of fire" (v 15). We will talk about the lake of fire in a moment, but the point is that if you are putting your trust in your own record, your own best efforts to be moral or religious or spiritual or patriotic, you don't stand a chance of acquittal, let alone of receiving eternal life. Your name must be found written in the book of life.

What is the book of life? It is the record of those who have been chosen by God and saved by Jesus. Elsewhere Revelation calls it "the Lamb's book of life, the Lamb who was slain" (13 v 8). The book of life catalogues the people of God rescued from their sins through the sacrifice of Jesus. Daniel predicted: "But at that time your people—everyone whose name is found written in the book—will be delivered" (Daniel 12 v 1).

Is your name in the book of life? *Are you sure?* Have you repented of your sin and cried out to God for mercy? When it comes to your eternal destiny, are your confidence and trust in Jesus and his death and resurrection, or is your trust in what you have done?

The lake of fire

Those not enrolled in the Lamb's book of life will face the lake of fire, the "second death" (Revelation 20 v 14). Simply put, the lake of fire is the most terrifying, horrific, awful place ever. It is hell, the final destiny of all those who oppose God and his laws, and who reject Jesus. Just a few verses earlier, we find this dreadful description of the lake of fire:

> And the devil, who deceived them, was thrown into the lake of burning sulfur, where the beast and the false prophet had been thrown. They will be tormented day and night for ever and ever.
>
> *Revelation 20 v 10*

Notice three things about the lake of fire:

- The lake of fire is the final judgment for God's enemies, including Satan and his followers, as well as death and Hades.
- The lake of fire is a place of conscious torment, not obliteration or annihilation. Its inmates are "tormented day and night."
- The torment of the lake of fire is eternal, lasting "for ever and ever."

As a pastor I have spoken to people facing their own mortality. And I have sometimes heard people say that they are more afraid of the process of dying than of actually being dead. But imagine a place where you are always dying but are never dead, always in torment but never relieved, always regretting but never forgiven, always ruined but never restored. No wonder Jesus described the lake of fire as the place of "weeping and gnashing of teeth." And as many Bible scholars point out, the descriptions of hell are likely figurative to some degree. The reality is probably even worse than the images suggest.

Whenever we ponder the nightmare of hell, a question inevitably arises. How could God inflict such punishment on human beings? Yes, we are all guilty sinners. But do our white lies, gossips, and drunken weekends really merit eternal damnation? It seems the eternal punishment of hell vastly outweighs the crimes of a finite lifetime, or even of a thousand human lifetimes!

Therein lies our problem. We don't have any sense of the gravity of our crime. The punishment does fit the crime, but we don't believe it because we don't appreciate the heinousness of the crime. We don't see how infinitely worthy and wonderful and glorious God is, and so we don't comprehend or feel how unmeasurably vile and unspeakably criminal it is to reject God or God's ways.

I heard a pastor friend describe the justness of hell this way during a sermon: imagine one boy punches another in a school-yard squabble. What happens to the hitter? Perhaps he stays after school for detention or is forced to write a letter of apology to his classmate.

Now imagine the boy gets mad in class and punches his teacher. What happens then? He would probably be expelled from the school for a time if not indefinitely. Go a step further and imagine our violent boy becomes a young man who punches a police officer. Now the reckless youth will go to jail for assault. And what if he degenerates further and attempts to attack a president or prime minister? The man will likely be killed on the spot by the security forces.

In all these cases the action is the same. The hypothetical assailant attacks another person. But the punishment for the attack escalates as the honor, dignity and importance of the victim grows.

What if the victim is someone infinitely worthy of honor and respect? Try to think of someone so awesome and marvelous that his very essence sets the standard for absolute good, beauty, and truth. To spurn and refuse such a being would be an infinitely evil crime, and would demand an equal punishment. That is what each of us has done! By disobeying God and living a life for our glory rather than his, we all stand guilty of an unendingly bad crime.

But here's the amazing news of the gospel: God not only sets the standard for goodness and truth, by which we are judged, but he also embodies the essence of love, by which we can be saved. God loved us so much that he sent his one and only Son to die on the cross as the substitute sufferer for our sins, and then rise again. Jesus came to rescue us from our worst problem, a problem far more disastrous than unemployment, divorce, depression, cancer or loneliness. Jesus rescued us from hell, the lake of fire, the second death. That's why Jesus told his disciples, after they returned from preaching, healing and casting out demons: "However, do not rejoice that the spirits submit to you, but rejoice that your names are written in heaven" (Luke 10 v 20).

How the new world will begin

If Jesus had only delivered his people from eternal ruin through his death and resurrection, it would still be the greatest news ever. But he did far more. Jesus not only saved us from something (the second death), but he saved us for something. He not only paid the penalty so we could be acquitted before the throne. He also granted to his people his own perfect record of obedience and love in order to qualify us for something greater. He took our sins and we got his righteousness. As a result, his followers will share in the new heavens and new earth, the new world that God will make.

> Then I saw "a new heaven and a new earth," for the first heaven and the first earth had passed away, and there was no longer any sea. I saw the Holy City, the new Jerusalem, coming down out of heaven from God, prepared as a bride beautifully dressed for her husband. And I heard a loud voice from the throne saying, "Look! God's dwelling place is now among the people, and he will dwell with them. They will be his people, and God himself will be with them and be their God. 'He will wipe every tear from their eyes. There will be no more death' or mourning or crying or pain, for the old order of things has passed away."
>
> *Revelation 21 v 1-4*

The end of this world is not the end of the story. After this current universe has passed away, after humanity has been sifted and sorted before God's throne, after all God's foes have been cast into the lake of fire to sink down forever under God's curse, then God will do something unimaginably wonderful. God will make a new heavens and a new earth.

At the center of this new creation will reside the New Jerusalem, the holy people of God fully prepared to be the perfect bride for Jesus. God's people will never again experience mourning or pain or death, nor will they ever sin again. And the best part of the new creation is that God himself will live with his people. It is God's presence that makes heaven so heavenly, and that will make the new creation the best place ever. In fact, Jesus defined eternal life as knowing God: "Now this is eternal life: that they know you, the only true God, and Jesus Christ, whom you have sent" (John 17 v 3). God's people will enjoy eternal life, because they will know God face to face.

Or to put it another way, the new heavens and new earth will be everything that hell isn't:

Lake of Fire	New Creation
weeping and gnashing of teeth	no more mourning or crying
eternal torment	no more pain
the second death	no more death / eternal life
punished for sin	made forever holy
dwelling with God's enemies	dwelling with God's perfected people
separated from God's saving presence	living with God / married to Christ

And if it is true that the reality of hell is far worse than the images the Bible uses to describe hell, then could it be that the new creation will be more wonderful than we can imagine, even when we meditate on the Bible's description of it? Could it be that our most sublime moments of joy in this life, and our highest experiences of God's reality in this world, are but shadowy glimpses of what we shall experience together when we live with Jesus in the new creation?

Have you ever sat in still wonder, watching a sunrise? Remember the feeling of the first time you fell in love? Have you ever sang in a church service where it felt that the Holy Spirit was filling your heart and shining on every face? Do you recall a holiday meal with family and friends filled with laughter and togetherness? What if all these experiences in this life are but an aroma of what God is cooking up for us in the new creation?

Jesus is coming! The world will end, humanity will be judged, and a glorious new world will begin. Let these great realities overwhelm you. Let them shake you to the core and drive you to throw yourself on the mercy of Jesus. And then let us join with the author of Revelation, in praying: "Amen. Come, Lord Jesus" (Revelation 22 v 20).

Chapter 6

How should we live until Jesus comes back?

What we think will happen in the future shapes our life in the present. We make decisions, spend money, and plan our calendars today in light of our assumptions about what will happen tomorrow. Chris buys stock in a company now because he believes it will perform well in coming months. Pat's work ethic today will likely vary based on whether she sees further career opportunities, or whether she believes she's working in a dead-end, low-paying job. And will John ask Jane out on a second date? It depends. Did he get any glimpse during the first date that the relationship might go somewhere?

My father died last year after an 18-year battle with cancer. Over that time he endured many surgical procedures and swallowed piles of pills—many of which had nasty side-effects. He did it because those treatments gave him hope of extended time with his family. And when the available medications finally gave no realistic chance of beating back the disease, he stopped treatment and courageously faced his final days, trusting in the Lord.

These kinds of possible future outcomes—economic forecasts, career opportunities, treatment options—all deal with future events in this world and they profoundly impact our choices. How much more should our understanding of the end of the world shape our present life? How should we live now in view of the ultimate future reality, namely, the return of Christ?

Jesus answered that question for us. He not only told us that he is returning, but he also told us what we should do in light of his return.

> Be careful, or your hearts will be weighed down with carousing, drunkenness and the anxieties of life, and that day will close on you suddenly like a trap. For it will come on all those who live on the face of the whole earth. Be always on the watch, and pray that you may be able to escape all that is about to happen, and that you may be able to stand before the Son of Man.
>
> *Luke 21 v 34-36*

Jesus' message was simple. Because he is coming back, you should "be careful" and "be always on the watch." Again and again, Jesus urged his disciples to be alert and prepared for the day of the Lord. Jesus told several parables to describe this state of readiness. In Matthew's Gospel, Jesus taught that his disciples should be like:

- a homeowner who stays awake at night so that he is prepared when a thief tries to break in (24 v 43-44).

- a servant who is hard at work doing his job when his master returns (24 v 45-51).

- bridesmaids who bring extra oil for their lamps so that when the groom appears at midnight they are ready to light their lamps and join the wedding procession (25 v 1-13).

- a servant who faithfully invests his master's money while the master has gone on a long journey (25 v 14-30).

In each parable, we find an example of a person being watchful, prepared and on mission at the moment when someone else important suddenly arrives.

But what exactly does it look like for us to be watchful, prepared and on mission awaiting Jesus' return? At the very least, a watchful Christian will be marked by the following:

Faith

Let's start with the basics. Because the world will end with Jesus' return as Judge, we need to repent of our sins and put our faith in Jesus now. And by faith, we mean more than just believing the concept that he's coming back. Faith means trusting in Jesus alone to save you, and it results in following him, whatever the cost. Jesus said:

> Whoever wants to be my disciple must deny themselves and take up their cross and follow me. For whoever wants to save their life will lose it, but whoever loses their life for me will find it. What good will it be for someone to gain the whole world, yet forfeit their soul? Or what can anyone give in exchange for their soul? For the Son of Man is going to come in his Father's glory with his angels, and then he will reward each person according to what they have done.
>
> *Matthew 16 v 24-26*

The most foolish mistake any person could make would be to ignore Jesus and only live for money or sex or retirement or fitness or recognition. How stupid to expend yourself for a world that's coming to an end, and yet refuse to follow the one who can save you in the end!

Jesus once mused: "When the Son of Man comes, will he find faith on the earth?" (Luke 18 v 8). Let's make that question more personal: when the Son of Man comes, will he find faith in us? In you? If you are reading this book and you haven't repented of your sins and trusted in Jesus, I pray that you would consider seriously how the world will end, and that you would call upon Jesus. And take heart, because "everyone who calls on the name of the Lord will be saved" (Acts 2 v 21).

Godliness

When we trust in Jesus, he doesn't merely save our souls on the judgment day. His saving grace transforms our lives now to be more godly, more like him.

> For the grace of God has appeared that offers salvation to all people. It teaches us to say "No" to ungodliness and worldly passions, and to live self-controlled, upright and godly lives in this present age, while we wait for the blessed hope— the appearing of the glory of our great God and Savior, Jesus Christ.   *Titus 2 v 11-13*

Waiting for the return of Jesus isn't like sitting passively in an airport terminal, counting the minutes until you get flown to another place. It's more like an athlete waiting for the tournament, or like an engaged couple waiting for their wedding day. That waiting is filled with active preparation. The athlete trains and drills and diets. And as the engaged couple waits, they book a reception hall, shop for dresses and tuxedos, and haggle over the guest list.

In the same way, those who await Jesus' return will be getting ready for life in the new creation, the home of righteousness (see chapter 5). They will be striving to kill sin and grow in Christ-like character. That's not to say that we achieve salvation on the judgment day by self-improvement in this life. Rather, the reality of our salvation reveals itself in a changing life now. Listen to how Paul connected our certain salvation and identity in Jesus with the need to grow in holiness:

But you, brothers and sisters, are not in darkness so that this day should surprise you like a thief. You are all children of the light and children of the day. We do not belong to the night or to the darkness. So then, let us not be like others, who are asleep, but let us be awake and sober. For those who sleep, sleep at night, and those who get drunk, get drunk at night. But since we belong to the day, let us be sober, putting on faith and love as a breastplate, and the hope of salvation as a helmet. For God did not appoint us to suffer wrath but to receive salvation through our Lord Jesus Christ. He died for us so that, whether we are awake or asleep, we may live together with him. Therefore encourage one another and build each other up, just as in fact you are doing.

1 Thessalonians 5 v 4-11

It is precisely because we have become children of light that we should live sober, awakened lives that won't be caught off guard by Jesus' return.

And did you notice that last sentence? We are to "encourage one another and build each other up." Pursuing godliness in light of Jesus' return isn't something we were meant to do alone. Growing in holiness is not a solo sport. Instead, think about your local church as your team, and your life in that church as team training. As you and fellow church members hear biblical teaching and worship together, as you pray and fellowship together, as you serve and encourage one another, you and the other children of the light are getting spiritually fit for the big event: the return of Jesus.

Prayer

Watching and being ready for Jesus' return should drive us to pray. The Bible links staying alert with praying. As we saw earlier, Jesus said: "Be always on the watch, and pray that you may be able to escape all that is about to happen" (Luke 21 v 36). Peter said: "The end of all things is near. Therefore be alert and of sober mind so that you may pray" (1 Peter 4 v 7).

Remember when Jesus prayed in the Garden of Gethsemane, just before he got taken away to be crucified? As he prayed late into the night, preparing himself for the coming trial, the disciples fell asleep. Jesus scolded them:

> Couldn't you men keep watch with me for one hour? ... Watch and pray so that you will not fall into temptation. The spirit is willing, but the flesh is weak. *Matthew 26 v 40-41*

Real prayer requires us to be physically awake and spiritually awake. What do we mean by being "spiritually awake?" It means, for example, that we are conscious of the ultimate value of God's glory and kingdom. And so in response we pray: "Your kingdom come, your will be done, on earth as it is in heaven." We pray for things on God's agenda like the salvation of lost people, the strengthening of our local church, and the work of missionaries.

Or, as in the case of the disciples in Gethsemane, when we're spiritually awake we recognize that we are in a spiritual battle against temptation and a tempter, and so we pray: "Lead us not into temptation but deliver us from evil." We ask God to strengthen us against our tendency to drunkenness or gossip or pornography or people pleasing.

Waiting for the return of Jesus can be tiring. We need the Holy Spirit's power to stay strong in faith and alert to temptation. How is your own practice of prayer? Are you awake and regularly communing with Jesus, or are you nodding off? Pray regularly with other Christians and keep each other awake!

Work

In his parables, Jesus compared the watchful Christian to a servant who is hard at work while the master is away. Before our master returns, we face the huge task of warning the world of Jesus' return and sharing the good news that this same Jesus will save anyone who repents and believes in him.

Back in chapter 2, we learned about some of the terrible things that will happen before Jesus returns, like false teachers, persecution, and wars. But it also included a promise about this gospel work. Jesus prophesied: "And this gospel of the kingdom will be preached in the whole world as a testimony to all nations, and then the end will come" (Matthew 24 v 14).

When the reality of Jesus' return and the end of the world grips us, it should spawn an urgency in our hearts to proclaim "this gospel of the kingdom" to all nations.

Faithful, alert servants participate intentionally in the work of proclamation. They pray for opportunities and boldness to share the good news. They invite friends to read the Bible with them. They give money to their local church and to missionaries to support gospel ministry. They pray for other churches and get excited about planting new churches. Some even give up a comfortable life in a familiar culture to live in another culture as a missionary.

This kind of behavior makes no sense to the world. It seems like a waste of time, resources and talent. But those who await the return of their Master see investing their lives for him as the most logical thing in the world.

Detachment

Living in light of Jesus' return leads not only to gospel engagement with the world, but also to a certain level of detachment from the world. If this world is going to end, then why cling to it desperately? Paul wrote to the Christians in the Roman city of Corinth:

> From now on those who have wives should live as if they do not; those who mourn, as if they did not; those who are happy, as if they were not; those who buy something, as if it were not theirs to keep; those who use the things of the world, as if not engrossed in them. For this world in its present form is passing away.
>
> *1 Corinthians 7 v 29-31*

Is Paul saying that Christians should divorce their wives or stop feeling emotions? Should we be like the Millerites, who believed Jesus was coming back in the 1800s and so sold their possessions and waited on mountaintops for the return of Christ?

No. This is not a call for all Christians to go and live in caves as hermits while they wait for Jesus' return. Rather, it is a call to avoid being engrossed in and absorbed with the world while still living in the world. Paul's point is that it makes no sense to make your life all about a world that's on its way out. It's like Jesus' warning: "Be careful, or your hearts will be weighed down with carousing, drunkenness and the anxieties of life, and that day will close on you suddenly like a trap" (Luke 21 v 34).

If you are Jesus' follower, you are a spiritual stranger and alien in this world. Do you approach earthly things like a pilgrim traveling light, or like a settler who's here to stay?

Hope

Finally, those who live in light of Jesus' second coming should be marked by an unsinkable hope. Jesus' return is a hope for Christians that far surpasses the worst that life can dish out. As Paul said: "I consider that our present sufferings are not worth comparing with the glory that will be revealed in us" (Romans 8 v 18).

Are we sick or disabled or plagued by mental illness? We have hope of resurrected bodies free of sickness and sorrow. Are we lonely? We await eternal fellowship with Jesus and his people. Are we weary of a world ruined by injustice and sin? God has promised us a new creation soaked with righteousness. When we trust in Jesus, we even find peace and confidence in the face of death.

This hope has propelled Christians through the centuries to suffer happily for the gospel. Jesus' followers have willingly embraced imprisonment, poverty, beatings, slander, ostracism and martyrdom, because they anticipate a glory that will more than make up for their losses in this life. As the missionary martyr Jim Elliot famously said: "He is no fool who gives up what he cannot keep in order to gain what he cannot lose." Those are the words of a man drunk on hope.

How should we live until Jesus comes back? Basically, we should live as Jesus lived during his own time on earth. When Jesus dwelt among us, he trusted daily in the Father, modeled perfect godliness and obedience, and prayed much. He rejected Satan's offers of worldly glory and instead set himself to the gospel work the Father had given him. That work led him to sacrifice his life on the cross to save us.

Until Jesus returns, let us imitate him. Let's copy his faith, holiness, labor and hope. "Let us throw off everything that hinders and the sin that so easily entangles. And let us run with perseverance the race marked out for us, 2 fixing our eyes on Jesus, the pioneer and perfecter of faith. For the joy set before him he endured the cross, scorning its shame, and sat down at the right hand of the throne of God" (Hebrews 12 v 1-2).

When is Jesus coming back?

Christians waiting for Jesus' return can't help but wonder: "When is he coming back?" Could it be in our lifetime? What if we are living at the end of the end times? In some ways it's healthy to think about him returning very soon, because it causes us to live more alertly.

But some have gone a step further and tried to pinpoint the year and even date of Jesus' return. These doomsday detectives typically piece together parts of prophecy from books like Daniel and Revelation, and sometimes correlate them with current events in order to pinpoint the date of the last day.

For example, William Miller predicted that Jesus would return some time between March 21, 1843 and March 21, 1844. Thousands of "Millerites" sold their possessions and waited for an end that didn't come. Edgar Whisenant released a short book entitled *88 Reasons Christ Will Return in 1988*. And, you guessed it, he had to revise his figures. He went on to predict Christ's return in 1989, 1993, and 1994. Some today see the establishment of the modern state of Israel in 1948 as a sign that Jesus will return within the lifetime of the generation alive in 1948. By the way, have you ever noticed that those who claim to know the time of Jesus' return almost always predict that it is in their own lifetime, and not hundreds of years in the future?

However, Jesus made it perfectly clear that no one knows when he is coming back, not even he himself: "But about that day or hour no one knows, not even the angels in heaven, nor the Son, but only the Father" (Matthew 24 v 36).

Some have suggested that while we cannot know the day and hour, we might be able to discern the year or general "season" of Jesus' return. Jesus also said:

> Now learn this lesson from the fig tree: As soon as its twigs get tender and its leaves come out, you know that summer is near. Even so, when you see all these things, you know that it is near, right at the door. Truly I tell you, this generation will certainly not pass away until all these things have happened.
>
> *Matthew 24 v 32-34*

Is this verse inviting us to figure out if we are in the final "season" before Christ returns?

Probably not. The phrase "this generation" almost certainly refers to the people to whom Jesus was speaking then, and not to us or a future generation.

What then are "all these things" (v 34) that must take place in that generation? It seems Jesus is referring to the terrible events from earlier in the chapter that Jesus prophesied would happen before his second coming (see chapter 2). In other words, Jesus was warning his disciples that the last days had finally arrived and that they would experience the trials that he predicted would happen before his second coming.

Could we be near the end now? It's certainly possible. Sometimes it seems that things couldn't get any worse. But others have thought the same about their generation. Why waste time and energy figuring out something that even Jesus doesn't know? Shouldn't we be alert and ready for Jesus no matter what? Christians should focus on the work at hand, and not on watching the clock.

Other titles in this series:

Did the devil make me do it?

by Mike McKinley

When Jesus walked the earth, he cast out demons and had powerful encounters with the devil. But who exactly is the devil, and where did he come from? And what is he up to in the world today? This short, readable book explains clearly and simply what we can say with certainty from the Bible about Satan, demons and evil spirits.

Who on earth is the Holy Spirit?

by Tim Chester and Christopher de la Hoyde

Many people find it easy to understand about God and Jesus, but struggle to understand quite how and where the Holy Spirit fits into the picture. Who exactly is he? And how does he work in our lives? These short, simple books are designed to help Christians understand what God has said in the Bible about these questions and many more.

Is forgiveness really free?

by Michael Jensen

Forgiveness is a free gift—not earned or deserved, we are told. But then the Christian life seems to have a long list of "dos" and "don'ts". So is forgiveness really free—or is it all a cosmic con trick?

This short, readable book explains clearly and simply what the Bible, and Jesus himself, says about grace, the law and what it means to be saved.

Is God anti-Gay?

by Sam Allberry

Christians, the church and the Bible seem to be out of step with modern attitudes toward homosexuality.

In this short, simple book, Sam Allberry wants to help confused Christians understand what God has said about these questions in the Scriptures, and offers a positive and liberating way forward through the debate.

Order from your local Good Book website:

UK & Europe: www.thegoodbook.co.uk
North America: www.thegoodbook.com
Australia: www.thegoodbook.com.au
New Zealand: www.thegoodbook.co.nz

thegoodbook
COMPANY
Opening up the Bible

At The Good Book Company, we are dedicated to helping Christians and local churches grow. We believe that God's growth process always starts with hearing clearly what he has said to us through his timeless word—the Bible.

Ever since we opened our doors in 1991, we have been striving to produce resources that honor God in the way the Bible is used. We have grown to become an international provider of user-friendly resources to the Christian community, with believers of all backgrounds and denominations using our Bible studies, books, evangelistic resources, DVD-based courses and training events.

We want to equip ordinary Christians to live for Christ day by day, and churches to grow in their knowledge of God, their love for one another, and the effectiveness of their outreach.

Call us for a discussion of your needs or visit one of our local websites for more information on the resources and services we provide.

UK & Europe: www.thegoodbook.co.uk
North America: www.thegoodbook.com
Australia: www.thegoodbook.com.au
New Zealand: www.thegoodbook.co.nz

UK & Europe: 0333 123 0880
North America: 866 244 2165
Australia: (02) 6100 4211
New Zealand: (+64) 3 343 1990